Arduino

The Essential Step by Step Guide to Begin Your Own Projects

Table of Contents

Introduction

Congratulations on downloading *Arduino: The Essential Step by Step Guide to Begin Your Own Projects* and thank you for doing so.

The following chapters will discuss some of the basics that you should know when you are ready to use the Arduino system. This is a great platform that works for beginners and experts who are ready to work on some new projects, who want to learn a new programming language, or who want to create a new robotics or electronic product.

Inside this guidebook, we will take a look at some of the steps that you should take when using the Arduino system. We will talk about some of the ways that you are able to use this platform and how it all got started. We will talk about some of the limitations and the benefits that come with this system and why you would choose the Arduino platform over other options.

Once we have some of the basics down, it is time to move on to how to what kinds of hardware you need, how to set up the free IDE to write the code, and even to hook it up to your computer no matter what kind of operating system you are using. Then we will move on to some of the projects that you are able to do with the Arduino system before ending with some of the tips and tricks that you should follow to make this platform really work for you.

When you are ready to learn how to work with electronics and robotics and you want to use a simple coding language to get this done, make sure to read through this guidebook and learn how the Arduino platform will be able to give you all the power that you need while also keeping things nice and simple.

There are plenty of books on this subject on the market, thanks again for choosing this one! Every effort was made to ensure it is full of as much useful information as possible, please enjoy!

Chapter 1: What is Arduino?

When it comes to creating some of your own robotics products, there are many things that you can consider. You will need to decide what kind of project you want to work on as well as the type of code that will help you to get the work done. One of the best options that you can use is the Arduino platform.

When we are talking about Arduino, we are talking about a software and microcontroller that is programmable, open sourced, and will use the ATMega chip. It is designed to be more of a prototyping platform, there is a huge fan base for this software when it comes to building an electronic project. When it comes to working with an electronic project, you will find that the Arduino platform is good for using either as a temporary addition while you work on the project or you can even embed it as a permanent part of the robotic project when it is done.

The Arduino board is also programmable with the Arduino software, which is pretty easy to use, even for those who are just getting started and have no idea how to work with this kind of software. If you have happened to use the C++ or Java programming languages, you will see that the Arduino coding language is going to be fairly similar. The idea behind using this software is meant to be really simple, but there is a lot of power there to, making it perfect for those who have some experience and for those who are just getting started out.

Arduino is also an open sourced platform, which means that anyone is able to use it, for free, as well as make adjustments to the code to fit their needs. This is a really cool addition for those who are just starting to use the Arduino system because they will be able to access thousands of codes from other programmers, or even make some changes to their own codes, in order to make the program work perfectly.

In addition to finding that many of the codes that you would like to use are already available and developed, beginners are going to enjoy that the Arduino community is pretty large. You will be able to go online and look through forums and communities to ask your personal questions related to your own project, to find out new information, and even watch tutorials to make working with Arduino easier than ever.

The Arduino platform may be pretty powerful to use, but it is also pretty basic. You will find that this platform only comes with two main components for you to use including:

- The hardware: this is going to include the microcontroller, which is also known as the circuit board. You are able to physically program this part. You will find that there are a number of Arduino boards for you to choose from and the choice will vary depending on the type of project that you are putting together.

- The software: this would be the environment that you use with the board, or the IDE, that is going to run right on your own computer. You will use the IDE to help you to upload and write the programming codes that you would like to be relayed over to the board. Once you write your programs on the board and transfer them over, the Arduino board should act in the manner that you requested.

These parts are able to come together to help you to get the project to work well. You need to make sure that you have some hardware in place, such as one of the Arduino board types, and then it needs to respond to what you are able to send through with the software. We will spend some time talking about the various things that you are able to do with the software in order to get your project to work later on, but both of these will need to be set up to ensure that the messages from the IDE are getting over to the board and working properly.

With Arduino, you need to have the IDE in place before writing out any code. The IDE for this program is free since it is open sourced, which makes it easier to get ahold of a copy. When writing codes, you will use the Arduino programming language, which will be easy to learn and works well with all of the operating systems on your computer.

One thing to note with the IDE and the coding language with Arduino, if you are working on a Windows 7 operating system or earlier, you will have a few steps that you will need to take, in addition to the regular steps, to make sure that the Arduino board will work with the operating system. It does work with the older versions of Windows, you just need to take some extra time to introduce the board to this system to get it to work.

Whether you are just getting started out with programming or want to use some of your skills to make a great electronic or robotic project, the Arduino platform will be able to help you get this done. It has all the power that you need with a simplistic background that helps even the beginner understand and accomplish what they want.

What can I do when using Arduino?

One of the first questions that you may have when you see the Arduino programming language is what you are able to do with it all? There are many programming languages out there and you are able to choose them to accomplish different things, but Arduino is going to work a bit differently compared to some of the others.

There are many great projects that you are able to do with the Arduino platform. Basically, the coding that goes with Arduino is going to travel from the IDE on your computer over to the hardware that you purchase to go with your project. You can use just the board or attach it to some electronic project to make it do some amazing things.

There are a lot of things that you can do with your robotics with the help of Arduino and if you are just getting started with your own electronic learning process or you want to try something new, this is the best platform to do so with. You are able to work with the board making sounds, blinking lights, sending out signals to control what is on the screen ahead of it, and so many other things. We will spend some time looking at the different projects that you are able to do with Arduino so you get a better idea of what you are able to do with this great language.

What isn't Arduino able to do?

As we mentioned above, there are quite a few things that you are able to do with the Arduino platform, but there are also some things that you won't be able to do. First, the Arduino language doesn't have a ton of processing power, so if you want to do a task that is considered intensive, you won't be able to do it with the Arduino platform. This means that the Arduino language won't be able to do things like output video or audio, or even record or process them, though you are able to use it to put graphics on a TFT or LCD screen. If you would like to do some of these processes, you would need to choose a different programming language.

In addition, you will find that the Arduino boards should work similar to a computer board, but this isn't true. It is not possible to hook up a webcam, keyboard, or other option to the board and try to use it because these boards don't have an operating system that comes with it. The confusion with this often comes from a similar product, the Raspberry Pi, which looks the same but actually has its own operating system and can work similar to a computer. The Arduino boards do not work this way.

When you write out the codes with this option, you are going to be using the operating system that comes with your computer. Once the code is written, it is not going to tell the computer what to do. Rather, your computer is going to send this code over to the Arduino board and the board will react in the manner that you wish. For example, you wouldn't be able to use this code to hack into another computer or to create your own website, but it can be sent over to the Arduino board to help it to become a remote control for a game.

Who should use Arduino?

One thing that you will like about the Arduino system is that anyone is able to use it for their own personal needs. Many experts in programming and robotics like to use Arduino because of all the variety that comes with it and they can create their own projects, make any changes to the code that they want, and it has enough power to get things done in no time. Beginners like this because it is easy to learn and you will be able to try out a few of the codes right away to create your own project.

Pretty much anyone who would like to create some of their own robotics and electronic projects will find that the Arduino system is one of the best for them to use. It has a lot of power that makes man projects possible but it is still easy enough that a beginner will not get too frustrated when trying to get it to work for the first time.

Why should I choose Arduino?

So far we have spent some time talking about what the Arduino platform is all about and why you would consider using it for your needs, such as what it is able to do. But there are some other choices out there that you can make when it comes to picking out a board that will control your electronic, so why should you choose to go with the Arduino platform? Here are some of the benefits that come with using Arduino and why you should choose this platform over one of the other options:

- Works across many platforms: the IDE that works with Arduino has the ability to work with pretty much any operating system that you want. It will work with Mac OS, Windows, and Linux. You do need to take precautions when using Windows 7 or earlier, but we will discuss later how to make this work even if you do have an older version.
- Simple environment: when you are a beginner, you don't want to pick an environment that is hard to get through. The Arduino environment is similar to the C++ environment, but has been made even simpler to use.
- Open source: the board plans that come with Arduino are published to be open sourced. This means that programmers

are able to come and use the platform and the software, as well as make changes to them whenever needed. This can be nice for programmers who are looking to use the platform but want to make some changes to get it to work for their needs and it is nice for the beginners because there are already many codes available for you to choose from.

- Free to use: since this is an open sourced software, the code is free to use. You will be able to use the software as well as the IDE for free, but keep in mind that you will need to purchase the boards that you want to use for your project. The boards are pretty inexpensive and there are a variety of options so you can experiment a bit and find the one that is right for you.
- A large community: the community for Arduino is pretty large, which makes it a great option for you to choose as a beginner. You will be able to find many forums and other locations where you can ask questions, look at tutorials, and find that answers that you need when working on your project.

There is so much that you are going to fall in love with when you are using this platform for some of your own projects. If you are just getting into the world of coding and you want to create a great project, or just mess around and learn something new, the Arduino platform is one of the best that you can choose. Let's take a look at some of the steps that you need to take to hook up one of the Arduino boards to your computer as well as some of the projects that you are able to do to get some great results with this platform.

Terminology to help out

When you are learning about a new coding language, there are always some new terminology that you will need to learn. Before we start to work on some of the projects that are later on in this book, we will need to discuss some of the terms that are popular in many of the directions so you know what is going on. Some of the terms that you should know include:

- Breadboard: this is a tool that is reusable for building circuits. It makes it easier to connect the circuits without having to get them permanently attached to the board. It is also a stable surface that will connect all your components together.
- Compiler: the compiler is a piece of software that will take your written program and translate it into something that the Arduino microcontroller is able to understand.
- Device driver: this is a piece of software that makes it so that the computer is able to communicate with the devices that are attached to it, such as the Arduino board. If the device driver doesn't work well, the computer and the Arduino board won't work together.
- EEPROM: this will stand for Electrically Erasable Programmable Read-Only Memory. This is a computer chip that will be written and re-written with the code that you want. You should notice that it is electrically erasable which is when an electric current will erase the information so that you are

able to use it. Keep in mind that all of the information on this will be erased when you use this option.

- External interrupt: the external interrupt means that something that is outside of the processor or the computer system and it needs your attention.
- Flash memory: this is one of your memory choices. It is going to retain the data whether there is power to the system or not. A good example would be the flash drive, which is going to store files, even if it isn't plugged into your computer.
- Digital input/output: digital pins are known to have either a high or a low value. You are able to pick from a wide variety of digital pins based on the type of board that you get.
- Analog input/output: this is opposite of working with digital. The analog is going to receive a continuous electrical signal, while the digital option will focus just on whether the value is either zero or one. Both can be available on your board depending on what you are doing with it.
- Processor: this is the part of the system that is going to take the instructions from the computer, figure out what you would like to have done with these instructions, and then runs them.
- Serial communication: when this kind of communication is occurring, it means that the two systems are sending digital pulses between them at a rate that you determine.
- Sketch: this is what the Arduino code is known as. It is going to consist of the instructions that you will send to tell Arduino

how to run. You will need to compile the sketch and then upload it to your board.

- SPI: this stands for serial peripheral interface. It is in charge of keeping the data communication protocol over small distances.

Getting started on one of your first projects in Arduino can be an exciting experience. This is a great program to learn how to use whether you are brand new to the world of coding or you are ready to take things to a new level. This guidebook will show you how to download some of your own projects and create them for the first time as well as some of the basics that you need to get the boards to work.

Chapter 2: Setting Up Your Arduino Platform

The Arduino platform is really popular and is always seeing a lot of changes, which means that as a beginner, there are always new things that you can learn about this platform in order to make it your own. We are going to focus on the basics that come with using the Arduino platform, but there are so many new projects that you can learn how to use with this option that it is a good idea to try new things out, keep up with some of the forums and communities, and see what is available for you to expand your knowledge with.

At this time, we will stick with the basics of how to use the platform as well as some of the projects that you are able to use. To get started, there are a few essentials that you will need to get ahold of in order to make the program work. These essentials include the Arduino board and the software that will talk to the board.

What is the Arduino Board?

The Arduino board is necessary if you would like to get started on your first project. There are a variety of options that you are able to choose from though and each one works with a different kind of project. This is why it is a good idea to understand some of the basics of the boards before you go out and purchase one, or you may end up with one that isn't what you want. Each board is able to do slightly different things and they may even look a bit different, but they should all have some of the same components in common including:

- Barrel Jack and USB: all of the boards that you can purchase will need to have some means in order to connect them to your power source, such as to the wall or to your computer. Many of them will also have a USB connect so that you are able to hook them to the computer and download the codes to it. You can also use the barrel jack which helps the board plug right into the wall.
- Pins: the pins are basically the points where you will create your circuits when you connect them with wires. There are several types of pins that you are able to use with the Arduino boards and each of them have a different function. There are several types of pins that you can find on your board including:
    - GND: this is the short for Gourd. These are going to be the pins that are used in order to ground out the circuit you are creating.
    - 5V and 3.3V: these are the pins that will give the right kind of voltage that your project needs, either the 5 volts or the 3.3 volts.
    - Analog: these are basically the pins that are seen right under the Analog In label on the board. These can be used for reading any signals that come in from the analog sensors and then they are turned into a digital value for you to read.
    - AREF: this is a short form of the Analog Reference. This is going to be the pin that you will use when you want to

set a maximum or an upper limit for the external voltage that goes to the analog pins. You will usually want to pick a maximum of 0 to 5 volts, but most of the time you won't use these at all.

- o PWM: these are found in many Arduino boards and this label is found right next to the digital pins. These pins are used for either normal digital pins or for a signal that is called Pulse-Width Modulation.
- o Digital: these are the pins that are fund right across from your analog pins and will be found right under the digital label. These pins are used to show the input and the output that is provided by the digital signal.

- Reset button: this is the button that is going to allow the pin to rest right on the ground and then will restart the code that you already loaded onto your board. It is the one that you will use when you want to test out your code a few times. Keep in mind that it is not going to reset everything on the board and it won't be able to fix issues if they are there.
- Power LED indicator: this is going to be a small LED light that should be right next to the label for ON right by it. This should light up whenever you plug this board into a new power source.
- Voltage regulator: this is the part of the board that will be able to control how much voltage you would like to get onto your board at a time. If there is voltage that is above this set limit, it will be able to turn it away. It will not be able to handle anything that is above 20 volts so make sure that your power

source is lower than this or you can have issues with destroying the board.

Each of these pins can be important based on the project that you are using your board for. You will need to pick out the board that has the right pins for the project that you need. Many of the beginner projects are going to have information on which board you are able to use and as you get more familiar with how things work, you will be able to figure out which boards are needed for your more advanced projects.

Hooking up the Arduino software

By this point, you will have the right hardware, or the right board, in order to get started with your first project. It is now time to install the software, also known as the IDE, to make sure that Arduino is going to work. The IDE is basically the environment that you need to have in order to write your code before sending it over to the board and to attach all of the circuit components. Without having the right IDE in place, you would never get the code over to the microcontroller and the board would just remain lifeless.

To download the IDE that you would like to use, go to the website www.arduino.cc in order to find the link for downloaded. Give the IDE some time to download on your computer, and when it is done, you should see a zip folder. Open up this file and then save it to the right location on your computer; pick the one that you like the best to ensure that you are able to find it later if needed.

When this is done, you can open up the Arduino.EXE file and then run it to get the installation started. There will be a few command prompts that will come up during the process so read through them and click in order to get it all set up. Once the IDE is installed and the components are all in place, it is time to start working on some of the projects in this guidebook in order to see what all Arduino is able to do.

Chapter 3: How the Layout Works on the Uno Board and Using the Arduino Library

When you are working with the Arduino platform, you will most likely use the Uno board. This is a great board to use and it will work for most of your beginner projects. It is the one that we will use for the projects in this book and you are sure to find that it works out well for your needs. In this chapter, we are going to talk about some of the layout that is available on the Uno board so that you are able to figure out where all the parts are before working on a project.

The Basic Layout

With the Uno board, there are 14 pins that are available to use and you can choose if they are the output or the input. The pins are then divided into three different groups, the Digital, the Analog In, and the Power. Each of these are important to making your project work.

The pins for Power are going to include the VIN pin which is for the voltage input, two GND pins (or grounds), and a 5V voltage source. Next are the 6 analog input pins and they are going to be numbered from A0 to A5. And then there are some digital pins that can be labeled from 0 to 13 depending on the board that you have. The pins that have the (~) symbol with them can be used as a PWM pin and the AREF, which is used to provide you with a reference voltage when you are using the analog input pins, and then there is the option for a Reset which helps you to reset your microcontroller when needed.

In addition to some of the pins that are discussed above, there are also some other pins that can be used for certain functions. The nice thing is that you are able to use these for multiple purposes, meaning that they aren't extra pins inside the board, but based on your project and how you are using the pins, they will do some amazing new things in the board. Some of the special purpose pins that you can use include:

- Serial: these are the 0 and 1 pins, which are used for any serial communication that you want to use. 0 is going to be used for receiving and the 1 is going to be used for transmitting.
- External interrupts: these are going to be the 2 and 3 pins, which are often set up to trigger a specific action based on the external conditions that come to the system.
- PWM: these are the 3, 5, 6, 9, 10, and 11 pins. These are often used for any output via the 8-bit while using the pulse-width modulation.
- SPI: these are going to be the 10, 11, 12, and 13 pins.
- LED: if you are working with LED lights on your project, you will need to use pin 13.

The pin numbers that are on the board are going to be the same numbers that you will see when you are creating new sketches on the Arduino board. Keep these in mind in case you need to use them for your projects.

The command library

Since this is a programming language, just like with working in Java or Python or one of the other options, there are going to be some commands that you will need to learn if you would like to interact with your board. We are going to take some time to look over some of the most common commands that are in the library and which you are most likely to use when creating a new project. Keep in mind that these are not all inclusive and there are many others that you may use depending on what you want your microcontroller to do.

Digital I/O Functions

There are three functions that can be used for the input and output of digital signals. One of them is to set the mode of your pin; this basically means that you will tell the pin whether it is going to be an output pin or an input pin. There is also the option to write on a pin to tell it whether it should be set as LOW or HIGH, and then there is one that is going to read through the status of the pin, such as if it is already set as LOW or HIGH so that you can make some changes.

Below, we are going to show the commands as well as some of the basic structures that go with them. The values are then going to be italicized are called the parameters and they are used to provide any information to the functions to help them to work in the proper way.

pinMode(pin, mode)

In this one, the pin number needs to end up being an integer value. Just pick the pin that you would like to use for this part and look at which number goes with it.

For this one, there are three possible modes that you can pick from include INPUT_PULLUP, OUTPUT, INPUT.

digitalWrite(pin, value)

For this one, the pin number also needs to be an integer value so just look up the number before proceeding.

The values for this one will either be LOW or HIGH so you will need to pick which one you would like to use.

digitalRead(pin)

For this one, the pin number needs to be an integer value just like it needed to be in the first place. Take a look at the pin that you would like to find information for and then place that number inside the brackets.

Since you are trying to get the information about a specific pin, you will get a value that is either LOW or HIGH.

Analog I/O

In addition to having pins that are for the digital inputs and outputs, there are also pins that are for analog. There are a few commands that you are able to use that work with the analog symbol as well based on what you would like to do with it. One of the commands is going to be used in order to set up the reference voltage, which is also used to be the maximum range of the input voltage. Another command that you are able to use is to read the analog voltage and then you can also be in charge of writing out the voltage for the analog pin that you choose.

Here are some of the analog commands that you may want to use when working on your code:

analogReference(type)

There are five options that are available for this one including:

DEFAULT: this is going to be either 3.3 volts or the 5 volts depending on the board that you pick from.

INTERNAL: this is a built in reference that will have some variances depending on the processor type that you choose to work with.

INTERNAL1V1: this is a built in that is on the 1.1V reference, but it is an option that is only going to be available when using the Mega.

INTERNAL2V56: this is the built in option that will come with 2.56V, but again, this is one that is only available on the Mega.

EXTERNAL: this one means that you are going to use the voltage that is applied to the AREF as the reference for the voltage that you will use.

analogRead(pin)

This is going to read whatever the voltage level is at the pin.

You will get an integer value that will show you what voltage is going through the analog pin that you are using.

analogWrite(pin, duty cycle)

This command is responsible for writing a PWM value right on the pin.

The duty cycle is then going to be somewhere between 0 and 255. The 0 means that the pin is always off and the 255 means that it is always on so there is usually some variance in between of this.

This is a good command to use when you would like to have an LED light that blinks on and off.

Learning how the board works and working with some of these commands that are already in your library can make a big difference in how your code is going to work. You need to learn where all the pins are and how the analog and the digital pins are going to differ from each other. Each of these is important to the code and which ones you use will really depend on the kind of project that you are working on and you may find that you need to work with several of them based on the project and the pins that you are working with.

Chapter 4: Programming Expressions on the Arduino Board

In the program, or in a sketch when dealing with arduino, you will need to use some expressions at some point. In a programming language, the expressions are combinations of logical operators, mathematical operators, constants, and variables. We are going to take some time to look over these different parts of the expressions and see how they are going to work inside of your code.

Data types and variables

The first part of the expression that we will talk about are the variables and data types. Variables are going to be like a label for Arduino because they are going to make it easier to associate certan values with their name. Before you are able to use a variable inside your sketch, you need to take the time to declare it out and this is where the data type will come in.The data type is going to tell the program what kind of data it should be able to find inside of your variable. Without a name or a data type, you will not be able to declare your variable in the Arduino sketch.

There are many data types that you will find inside of your Arduino sketch, but some of the most commonly used types include:

- Boolean: these are the true or false data types or the 1 and 0 type. It will look at the expression and figure out if the answer is true or false. If the answer is true, it will give one result and if it is false, it will give another result.

- Characters: these are the letters or numbers that are used inside the code. For example, you could have a character like 'A' or 'a' or you could have integer numbers that are from -128 to 127.
- Int: these are the integer numbers. In Arduino, they can fall between -32768 to 32767.
- Long: these are another type of integer numbers and they can fall between =2157483648 to 215483647.

Declaring these variables can be pretty easy inside of Arduino. For example, let's say that you have a variable called ledPin and you want to declare it. We are going to give it an int data type with a value of 5. The way that we would declare this is:

```
int ledPin = 5;
```

And it is as simple as that. Make sure to add in the semicolon at the end as this is good programming practice and helps the IDE to read through and run the sketch exactly the way that you wrote it out.

Operators

Another thing that you can work with inside your sketch is the operators. These are often used in order to manipulate your variables. For some programming languages, there are a long list of operators that you can use, but for Arduino, there are going to be four main ones that you can work with including Boolean, logical, mathematical, and assignment operators. Let's take a look at each of these and learn how they work.

- Assignment operators: this one is going to use the equal sign (=) in order to calculate the final value of the data type that is on the right hand side of the sign. It is also going to associate the value on the right side to the variable that is on the left hand side of your sign.
- Mathematical operators: these are the ones that you are going to use if you want to do some kind of mathematical equation inside of your code. They would include the signs (+), (-), (*), (/), and (%).
- Logical operators: these are also good if you would like to compare some things together. You can use the (==) operator to mean equal to, (!=) for not equal to, (>) for greater than, < for less than, <= for less than or equal to, and >= for greater than or equal to.
- Boolean operators: these operators are only going to work with boolean data types. This means that the data type needs to be either 0, 1, true, or false. These would include the (!) for not, (||) for or, and the (&&) for and.

There are also operators that work in decrements and increments. These would include the signs (++) and (--). If you place the (++) after the name of the variable, such as writing out x++, you will just add 1 to the value of x. If you use the (--) after the name of the variable, it will simply subtract 1 from the value of x.

Expressions:

So when you are working with expressions in this sketch, you will just be able to combine together a few of the different types of the data types that were listed above. When these come together, you will find that you are able to get the code to do some amazing things. For example, a simple mathematical expression in this code would include something like a = 2*3-5. The compiler, which is the thing in the program that will translate the instructions that you write will see your assignment operator, or the (=), so it will first look over to the left to see what operation is there and then the order that it will need to be processed.

With the example that we had above, the compiler is going to use the MDAS rule. This basically stands for multiply, divide, add, and substract. This is the order that you would do things inside of the code so that the right answer is found. So for this example, the compiler would do the multiplication first and end up with 6. Since there isn't any division or addition in this answer, it will skip over to subtraction and take 5 from the 6 to give you an answer of 1.

This is going to be true with all of the mathematical expressions if you end up having more than one mathematical operator inside of it. If you happen to have more than one of the same symbol, such as if the equation above was a = 2*3-5*3, you would need to do the multiplication parts first, ending up with 6-15 with an answer of -9. This is the same no matter how many of the mathematical equations that you end up with.

The logical expressions are the ones that will use the logical operators and the Boolean operators and they are actually used quite a bit within your Arduino sketches. Let's look at an example where you would like something specific to happen if the pin 1 is HIGH or if pin2 is HIHG. You would be able to create a conditional statement in order to get this to happen and you would need to use the logical operator.

For this conditional expression, you would write out something like the following: (pin1 == HIGH || pin2 == HIGH). As you can see, the (||), which is one of the logical operators, is in use, which means that if either the first or the second condition is true, the entire expression is going to be considered true. If you would like to have both of the pins to be at HIGH before the event happens, you would change the conditional expression to be something like the following: (pin1 == HIGH && pin2 == HIGH).

There are many different ways that you would be able to use the different data types inside of your code to get them to work the way that you would like. These are pretty easy to work with and you can mix and match them to get the code, or the sketch, to work in the way that you would like. Try out a few of them in your own IDE and see how the compiler reacts or look at some of the examples that are later in this guidebook and see how many of the data types that you can recognize and how they work in different scenarios.

Chapter 5: The Structures of Programming in Arduino

Next we are going to talk about the basic programming structures that are found inside of the Arduino platform. There are three of them that you will be able to use to make a difference in your sketches and these include repetition, decision, and sequential.

The first one is the sequential structure and these are considered some of the easiest. Inside of these structures, the instructions are going to be performed in the exact order that they appear inside your program. If you place an instruction at one pont of the code, it is going to show up on the board in the exact same order. A lot of the codes that we will write out in this book will work in this manner to keep things easier.

Decision structures are another type that you would be able to use inside of your sketch and they are also known as branching structures. These are important because they are going to allow the computer to select what instructions are going to be sent over based on a condition that you set. These are a bit more complex, but can open up a lot of things that you are able to do inside of your code.

And finally, there are the repetition structures. These are the good ones to use any time that you would like to have the same block of code or instructions to repeat. They will keep repeating the same instructions until your stopping condition shows up and is met.

We are going to spend some more time talking about how these structures are going to work and even the best way that you are able to use them in your sketches. Each of them have their place in your sketch and it depends on what you would like to have happen inside the sketch, such as what you need for your particular project.

Decision structures

First on the list is the decision structures. Remember that these are the ones that are going to give the computer permission in order to select the instructions that will be sent over to your board based on the conditions that are set by the programmer and the input that the user gives.

There are a number of forms for the decision structure, but the most basic one is the if statement. Here is an example program of how the if statement would work:

```
if (buttonStatus == HIGH){
        digitalWrite(ledPin, HIGH);
}
Else{
        digitalWrite(ledPin, LOW);
}
```

In this example, the if block is going to extend from where the "if" word shows up in your code and it goes all the way through until it reaches the last curly brace. The condition that will determine which of the instructions that are allowed to run is the buttonStatus == HIGH part. If the computer finds that this is a true condition, then we set the ledPin to HIGH, which will make the LED light show up. If the computer determines that the condition is not true, it will determine that the condition is false. This is where we are going to set the ledPin to LOW, which will turn off the LED light.

This can work in many different ways to turn lights on and off inside your code or even to help with turning music on and off among other things. Let's take a look at another example and see how this can work.

```
if (value < 10) {
        digitalWrite(ledPin, HIGH);
}
```

This example is a bit simpler to understand because it just has one part to the whole thing rather than the two statements that we had above. This one is only going to show up the LED light if the condition is true. Nothing is going to happen if the condition is not true, which is basically the same thing as before, but worked out in a different way. For this example, if the value in the program is greater than or equal to 10, there will be nothing that happens. But if the value ends up being less than 10, the ledPin will be set to HIGH and hte LED light will show up.

Repetition Structures

Next on the list is the repetition structures. Remember that these are the ones that will continue to send out the same section of instructions over and over again until you put in a stop feature that will make it go on to the next set of instructions if there are any. For example, you could set this up so that the LED light keeps on blinking on and off until there is something else that stops it, rather than with the previous code just having the light blink on and off once. There are many ways that you would be able to use a repetition structure inside of your code so let's take a look.

For this example, we are going to assume that we want the pin3 to have a HIGH value before anything happens. So as long as the pin 3 has this value of HIGH, we will want to keep the LED light off. We would do this with the following code:

```
while (digitalRead(3) == HIGH){
        digitalWrite(ledPin, LOW);
}
```

This is an example of the while block and it is going to start with the "while" word and will keep on going through the code until that last curly brace, even if you add in a few other things to this. Everything that is in between the curly brace sin this code will repeat until the value of pin 3 is no longer the same as HIGH.

The while block is just one tpe of repetition structure that you are able to use in this type of code. You can also choose to use the for loop. These are going to be used when you are able to determine ahead of time how many times you want that segment of code to run for you. For example, if you want to write out a code that needs to allow the LED light to blink 10 times, you would be able to use the for loop.

So let's say that we would like to make sure that the same block of code is repeated the 10 times. We would need to use the following sketch to help make this happen:

```
for (int count = 1; count <= 10; count ++) {...}
```

In this code, we need the variable to keep track of how many times your loop has already been done. We set the whole thing up so that the integer variable named count. The count will start with the value of 1 and then it will add to it each time that it goes through the loop, finally stopping when it reaches ten times. Keep in mind this is going to work best if you already know how many times you need the loop to run. If you are uncertain about how many times the loop should run or you would just like it to continue going until the conditions are no longer met, you would want to go with an option like the while block instead of the for loop above.

In addition to what we have discussed, we also need to set up a condition to help the code determine if the loop should keep on going. In this example above, the condition is the <= 5. Once the count gets above, or greater than, 5, your loop is going to stop. Now you may be wondering what is keeping the compiler from always assuming that it is counting the first time through and getting stuck at a value of 1. The command of ++ that we added in will make sure that each time it adds one more to the value until you get above 5.

So, there are a few things that go into play to show how the for loop is going to work. Some of the things that you should keep in mind with the for loop when you want to use it include:

- The for loop is going to create a variable named count and then it will give it a data type integer with the initial value of that integer being 1.
- The for loop will be able to run the instructions that are inside the body of your loop, which is the same as the information that is inside of your curly braces.
- The for loop will bea ble to add one to the count that you have when you insert the count command. Remember that the count command is ++.
- The for loop is able to check the new value of the count and then compares it to the condition count. In this example, it will compare the new value count to the condition <= 5.

- With the for loop, as long as your new value count is still <= 5, the information that is inside the loop will continue to run again.
- When working with a for loop, once the new value is no longer <= 5, such as the new value being 6 or more, the program will stop going through the loop. If there are some more instructions in place that come after yur curly braces, the program will continue on and execute those commands. If this is the final or only command in the series, it will stop at this point.

These structures are important ones to learn because they carry a lot of importance in the codes that you are trying to create. Whether you are looking to make sure that the light switches on in your controller or you would like a certain song or sound to repeat a few times throughout, you will find that learning how to do the controls above will really help to make things easier. Bring out your Arduino IDE and try out a few of the examples above with your board to see how they will work and to get a feel for these inside your own code.

Chapter 6: Testing Out Arduino and Trying Out a Few Codes

Once you have had some time to set up the IDE and other software that you need to use with Arduino and you have taken a look at some of the boards that you are able to use with your projects, it is time to get everything set up and test out the boards and the software a bit to see how they work. In this chapter, we will actually start out with a few of the projects that you are able to do with the help of the Arduino boards and software. This may seem a little bit intimidating in the beginning, but you will see that Arduino is really easy to use and you will be able to make some of these projects happen in just a few minutes.

Getting started on the first project is not difficult. You just need to have the right code, make sure that the computer is able to recognize the hardware that you are using (which in this case would be the Arduino board that you picked out) and have the IDE all set up. Once all of this is in place, you are ready to start working on some of the basic projects.

First, let's think about the code. If you have already worked with the C++ coding language, you are off to a good start. This coding language is similar to what you will find with the Arduino language so this will make things easier. Don't worry if you haven't worked in C++ in the past; this is a simple language and with the help of our codes in this book, you will be able to figure it out to get the hardware to do what you would like.

Next, you need to get the IDE set up for Arduino. You will find that it is really difficult to get the code written out and sent to the hardware if you don't have the right IDE running the way that it should. The IDE is basically the environment, which will look like the screen on your computer that is needed in order to write the codes. When you write out the codes inside the IDE, it is going to be able to read through it and then process it before translating over to the Arduino board. This is a simple step and you can download the IDE for free online, but make sure that you aren't skipping out on it or you will have some issues later on.

Now that you have the IDE set up for Arduino and you have the hardware in place, it is time to do a bit of testing to make sure that the program is going to work well. This is a good way to make sure that everything is working properly and gives the beginner a chance to mess around with the IDE, the code, and the hardware to see how it is all going to work for them.

In our first example, we are going to use the Arduino UNO (R3) board to get things to work (you are able to make some modifications if you would like to use this on a different board, but this is the board that we are going to use for this demonstration). In addition to the circuit board that we talked about above, you will also need the following in order to finish up this project:

A computer: you should make sure that the computer is relatively new. It doesn't have to be brand new to work, but something that is newer than fifteen years for example will help. The computer should also have either the Mac operating system, Linux, or a Windows XP or above operating system.

A USB cable: the A to B one is the best because it allows you to connect the Arduino board over to the computer. You can also just pick out any USB cable that you would like that fits into the computer as well as to the board so that they work together.

An LED: this is important for the project we will do next so make sure that you have one that is able to work with your Arduino board.

When you have these items all gathered and ready to go, you will be ready to start testing out and learning how to use this system for your electronic and robotic projects.

Getting the board to plug in

In most cases, you will be able to use the USB cord mentioned above in order to connect the Arduino board over to the computer, but you are also able to use another power supply, such as one that plugs it into the wall with the help of a barrel jack. If you would like to make sure that the board is working with the IDE for Arduino, you will need to make sure that the board is hooked into the computer rather than the wall. Once you have had a chance to upload your programming over to the Arduino board from the IDE, you can take it from the computer and use the wall power supply if that is easier for you.

So you now need to bring out your USB cable and use it to connect your board with the computer. Once these are connected together, you should take a look at the board and look for the ON light. It should be blinking pretty quickly. This is the default program that is on the board and is stored inside on the chip. The project we are going to do a bit later on is going to override this default program and make it so that your LED light is able to blink off and on at a much slower space, we'll leave two seconds between each of the blinks, rather than the rapid pace that is set up on the board.

If the light is not blinking at all at this time, you may need to check that it is plugged in the proper way. The USB cable may not be inside the machine the proper way or you are using the wrong cord. Make sure to check that these are both right and see if that helps the light to come on and start blinking at a quick pace.

Install your drivers

One the Arduino board is hooked up with the computer, it is time to install the drivers that you will need to make the program work. If you are working with a Windows 7 computer or earlier, you will need to do the following steps to make sure that the system will recognize the board that you are doing and you will need to do this each time you bring out a new board. For Linux, Mac OS, and Windows 8 or higher operating systems, you can skip over these steps because the system will already be able to recognize the board.

For the earlier versions of Windows, follow these simple steps in order to install the right drivers onto the computer so that the codes get sent out to the Arduino boards:

- Once you have the board plugged into your computer, the Windows system is going to start with the process of installing the driver. Keep an eye on this because after just a few minutes, the process is going to fail on you.
- After the process has failed, you will need to go to the Start Menu and then click on your Control Panel.
- Take some time to go through the Control Panel until you find where System and Security are. Click on your System Tab.
- Once this window is up, you will need to click on the Device Manager in order to pen it up.
- Now you look under the Ports. You should be able to see that there is an open port called Arduino UNO (COMxx). If you notice that the Ports section doesn't show up on the device, look under the Other Devices and then search for Unknown Device.
- Right click on the device and then choose the Update Driver Software option.

- Finally, you should look for and select the file called Arduino.inf, which you should be able to find inside of your Drivers folder for the Arduino Software download. If you happen to have an older version of the Arduino IDE, this file may be called Arduino UNO.inf instead.
- At this point, your Windows system will be able to finish up the process for installation without any more help from you.

Remember that with these steps, you are only going to need to do them if your Windows operating system is a bit older. If you are using Linux or the Mac OS or you have Windows 8 or newer, you will not need to do these steps. The newer operating systems are already set up in order to work with the IDE and they are able to recognize the Arduino board that you are using without needing to do all the other steps.

This means that with the other operating systems that you are using, you can just use the USB in order to hook the board with the computer and you are all set to go. The newer operating systems are able to recognize the device and you can get to work right away!

Working on a launch and sketch with Arduino

Once the board is hooked up to the computer and you have the right IDE installed, it is time to do a quick test drive of your board using our first program. This first program is going to help you to learn how to use the Arduino programming language, which is helpful for those who are not familiar with using it and it ensures that the board and the IDE are going to work properly for any other projects. Before we start with this, there are a few pointers you should understand before you write out your first code with Arduino.

First, the codes inside of Arduino are called sketches and you will be using the C++ language in order to write them out. If you already know how to use the C++ language, this is going to be even easier to work on the first program. Even if you aren't used to working with the C++ code, you will be able to figure out how to work on these codes pretty easily.

Every sketch that you work on will need to have two void functions that aren't allowed to return a value and these include the setup() and the loop() functions. The setup() method is going to run through the sketch just once, right after you have powered up the Arduino board and gotten it to start. And then the loop() method is the one that will continue on until you take the board and unplug it from the computer. During the setup() part of the sketch, you will want to make sure that all of the initialization steps are taken care of and then with the loop() you are going to place in the code that you would like to have run over and over again with your board.

Let's take a quick look at some basic code that can be used within this language and which will work on your board:

void setup(){

}

void loop(){

}

This is one of the most basic syntaxes that you are able to use and if you took the time to type this into your IDE, nothing would happen at all. You will need to add in just a few more parts to your code to get it to behave the way that you would like, but this syntax is a good example of the basics that you need in order to lay out the code in Arduino.

Now that you know some of the basics that come with writing the code with Arduino, it is time to get started on the rest of the steps for your first program. The steps that you need to make this happen include:

- Make sure that you plug the Arduino board into your computer and that you have the Arduino application launched.
- Open up the Blink example sketch. You will be able to find this sketch by clicking on File, Examples, 1_Basics, Blink.
- You will then need to select on the board type that you would like to use on this project. To make this selection, you just need to click on Tools, Board, and then click on your board type.

- At this point, you can choose the COM or the serial port based on what Arduino is attached to. You will be able to do this by clicking on Tools, then Port, and then COMxx.

If you are unsure about which serial device you have on the board, you can look at all of your ports that are available and see if you are able to figure out the number. If you are still confused about which one is yours, you can take the board out of the computer and then see which port disappears when the board is all gone. This is the one that you will need to use for this first step.

Uploading and getting the light to blink

If you unplugged the board in the previous step, you need to get the board back and connected to your computer with your Blink sketch open. Now you should press on the Upload button. Wait a few seconds and then look to see if the LEDs for the TX and R are flashing while your program is uploading to the board. If this particular upload ends up being successful, you should be able to look on the computer and see that the status bar of your Blink Sketch will say Done Uploading.

If the process was done correctly, the LED light for ON, which should be an orange light, will start to blink slowly rather than in a rapid manner like it was doing earlier. At this time, you have finished programming the first thing on this board. As you can see, working with the Arduino board is pretty simple and it can be as easy and fast as the example that we just did for slowing down the LED ON light.

What if this doesn't work?

For the most part, you will be able to run the steps that we discussed above and the light is going to change from a fast blink to one that is slower. But there are times when it isn't going to work as well for you. Maybe the light turns off completely or it doesn't stop blinking at all. There are a few things that could be causing some of these difficulties with your system. Some of the troubleshooting that you can do to make this better include:

Go back through and see if you selected the right board type when starting. If you picked the wrong kind of board, you will find that the code isn't going to work. Remember that if you are using a board that is different than the one we are using in the book, you will need to select that one instead. You can go back to the Tools and then Board and make sure that the right board has been selected.

Next, you should double check that you are using the right port. You can go through and select the Tools and then Serial port menu. Double check to see if you are using the right port so that the code can be sent through.

Another thing to check is to see if your drivers on the board are installed properly. You should visit Tools and then Serial Port inside the IDE while your board is connected. If everything is hooked in right, you should notice that there is an extra item inside the IDE that wouldn't be there before the board was plugged in.

Checking on these things should help to troubleshoot most of the issues that you are going to have with getting the light to slow down on the Arduino. If one of these is the problem, you should be able to see that the ON light is going to work at the slower blinking speed once you give one of them a try. If you find that the first option doesn't work, you can go down the list and try each of them out.

Light up the LED

At this point, you have an Arduino that is active so now it is time to work with it a bit more while working on your second project. This is a good one for those beginners who haven't had experience with circuitry in the past because it brings this into the mix to change how some of the lights are going to work. For this one, you need to make sure that the Arduino is launched and that the LED is ready as well. Once these two things are set up, make sure to follow these easy steps to work on the second project:

- First, plug in the board to your computer.
- Now you can open up another sketch example. To do this, just click on File ,Examples, Basics, and BareMinimum. This will open up in a brand new window that will have your simple sketch in place. This is basically the framework for this new program.

- You can then connect in the anode of the LED, putting in the pin that is longer to the pin 13 that is on your board and then the cathode, or the shorter pin, into the GND pin that is adjacent.
- Go back to your sketch and work on the setup() part. Add in the code *pinModel(13, OUTPUT)*. This is the command that will run just once so that the board is configured properly and to ensure that it is ready to do the program.
- Now you can work on the loop() method of our code. In this area, you will write out the code *digitalWrite(13, HIGH)*. This is going to set it up so that the pin 13will become the output pin that has the high voltage level.

So when all of this is said and done, you will have the following code written out in your sketch to tell the program what you want to get done:

void setup(){

pinModel(13, OUTPUT):

}

void loop(){

digitalWrite(13, HIGH):

}

When you put this into the compiler and then hit the Upload button, you will just need to wait a moment or two. Then the Done Uploading message is going to show up in the IDE in the status bar. When this status bar comes up on the screen, take a look over at your Arduino board and see if the light for the LED shows up. If this does show up, you were successful with completing this process the right way!

And with that you are done with your very first two projects using the Arduino board. As you can see, they are pretty simple to learn and even if you don't have any coding experience from the past, these are easy enough to learn how to do. We will take a look at a few other projects that you can work on in the next few chapters, but try out these first two simple projects first and see how easy it can be to get started with your own Arduino board.

Chapter 7: Working on an LED Light Up Strip

The projects that we discussed above were perfect for helping you to get used to the Arduino board and software and can help you to work out some of the kinks about how it all works before going any further. If you took the time to try out those projects above, you are really ready to move on and work on something that is a bit more complex. This chapter will start out with some more of the basic projects that you may want to try out. While the codes are going to be a bit longer than before and may take a bit more time to process through between the IDE on your computer and your Arduino board, they are definitely going to help you to make some amazing products.

As a beginner, you may feel that you won't be able to do some of these projects on your own simply because you don't have the experience and they seem a little bit scary and long. Don't worry, Arduino is simple and if you are just able to use the codes that come with each of the projects and you have the right tools in place (which we will list out at the beginning of each project), you will find that these projects don't have to be so difficult. By the time you are done with this chapter, you will be able to work on things like an LED light up strip and even a heated blanket! So let's get started on creating some more great projects with our Arduino system.

LED light up strip

The first thing that we are going to create in this chapter is going to work with e-textiles and it can be really fun and simple to learn. We are going to create a simple Lily Pad Arduino LED light-up. The supplies that you are going to need in order to create this project include:

- An embroidery hoop
- Fabric
- Conducting thread bobbin
- Needle threader
- Coin cell battery
- A Lily Pad coin cell battery holder
- Needles
- A rainbow LED strip
- Scissors

Once you have all the supplies in place, you can take the needle and thread it through with the conductive thread. You can also use the embroidery hoop to set your fabric to make it taught and a bit easier to use. Make a positive trace, which basically means make a mark that leads from the power supply over to the positive side of your LED strip. This positive trace is going to get started right from the battery pack. You can place your battery pack, making sure that the battery is not in there yet, near where you want to place the LED, but make sure that one hole with a plus and one with a negative are pointed towards the location of your LED. These will be considered the positive pins and the negative pins in the battery back.

Once your battery pack is in the right place, you can work on the sewing process. You will first want to trap the edge of the board with your fabric and you would do this by wrapping it in thread, three or four times, on each of the positive pins on your board (you should see that there is a second positive pin on the top of your board). When you are sewing these pins, you will want to do some smaller stitches rather than just a big long stitch because these smaller ones will help the pack to stay nice and tight. A big stitch may seem like the best option, but it allows the stuff to move around and the circuits could short out.

Take your time to stitch this thread all the way through the positive side of the LED strip, sewing it down like your other positive spin. At some point, check to make sure that you are using the right pole because if you thread up on the wrong side, you will not be able to get the LED light to show up.

Once the positive side is done, it is time to work on your negative trace. This is going to return from the current side of your strip of LED to the negative side of the pack. You are basically going to use the same steps as we did before, but you are just going the opposite way this time until you reach the end.

When the sewing is done, you should look over the project and make sure that the thread isn't dangling at all throughout the project. Also check to see if the positive and negative traces are not touching any other parts because this could cause some issues with the light working.

If everything looks good and you got the sides sewed together properly, you can now take the battery and place it into the pack. The LED should light up right away once the battery goes inside. Congrats! You have just created a new project as an e-textile with the help of the Arduino circuit!

Chapter 8: Creating Your Own Heating Blanket

For this chapter, we are going to work on making one of our own heating blankets. This is a great project if you are dealing with those cold winter nights and want to stay nice and warm. This project is really neat, but you don't have to worry about it becoming too difficult. You already have the right software and hardware in place to make your own heating blanket and once you see how easy this process is, you are sure to want to make one for everyone in your home.

To get started on this project, there are a few supplies that you will need. The supplies that are needed to make your own heating blanket include:

Red hook up wire

Lily Pad Arduino board

A wall adapter for power supply (5V DC 1A)

N-Channel MOSFET 60V 30A

2 5X15 Heating pads

Switch

Conductive thread

Lily Pad LED light

Black hook up wire

Now that you have all of the supplies that you need, it is time to get started on your project by following these steps:

- First, take the hand warmer blankets and sew it up. You should use your creativity to make this look the shape that you want. As a beginner you may want to keep it simple and just sew up the blanket in a square, or you can be creative and sew it up another way.

- Once the blanket is ready, it is time to work with the conducting thread. This is going to work in a similar manner that you did with your first project, using the conducting thread to get the board connected and then sewing to conduct the edges to the positive side where the blue LED lights are located. You also need to sew together your negative sides as well.

- Now take your wire for hook up, the one that is red, and then connect the positive contact of your board with the positive side of your switch. You should use the connection that is parallel in order to connect these at the same time to the positive part of the heating pad. Be careful to watch that you are soldering this connection rather than using your conductive thread.

- After you have the positive sides hooked up, it is time to connect the negative parts. You will need to use the black hook up wire and connect the negative parts of the board over to their corresponding parts of the power source. You can then connect both of these over to the negative parts of the switch.

- You can work next on creating a parallel connection that goes to the S leg of the MOSFET.

- It is time to create an additional parallel connect that will go to your 10K resistor.

- Hook up your 11th pin on your board over to the leg that says G on the MOSFET, making sure that this branch is able to go parallel to the opposite end of the resistor.

- Connect the leg that says D of your MOSFET to the negative contacts on the heating blanket.

At this point, you have all of your parts connected together. It is time to bring up the IDE for the Arduino on your computer and write out the proper code to make the blanket work. The code that is needed to turn on the Arduino board and to make the blanket turn on includes:

language: C

/*

Hardware Connections:

-led1 = D9;

```
-led2 = D10;

-led3 = D11;

-button = D2;

-Mosfet = D3;

*/

int btnPin = 2;

boolean btnPressed = false;

int fetPin = 3;

int led1 = 9;

int led2 = 10;

int led3 = 11;

int mode;

void setup(){

// initialize the digital pin as an output.

pinMode(btnPin, INPUT);

pinMode(fetPin, OUTPUT);

pnMode(led1, OUTPUT);

pinMode(led2, OUTPUT);
```

```
pinMode(led3, OUTPUT);

}

// the loop routine runs over and over again forever:

void loop(){

// increment mode on depress, unless mode = 3, then reset to 0

if (btnPressed && digitalRead(btnPin) == LOW)

mode = mode == 3 ? 0 : mode + 1:

// Assign button state

btnPressed = digitalRead(btnPin):

switch (mode)

{

        case 0:

        analogWrite(fetPin, 0); // off

        digitalWrite(led1, LOW)

        digitalWrite(led2, LOW)

        digitalWrite(led3, LOW)

        break;

        case 1:
```

```
analogWrite(fetPin, 85); // 33% duty cycle

digitalWrite(led1, HIGH);

digitalWrite(led2, LOW);

digitalWrite(led3, LOW);

break;

case 2:

analogWrite(fetPin, 170); // 66% duty cycle

digitalWrite(led1, HIGH);

digitalWrite(led2, HIGH);

digitalWrite(led3, LOW);

break:

case 3:

analogWrite(fetPin, 255); // 100% duty cycle

digitalWrite(led1, HIGH);

digitalWrite(led2, HIGH):

digitalWrite(led3, HIGH);

break;

}
```

}

Right now, you are probably looking at the code and thinking that it is really long. While it does take some time to type in, this is necessary to give the board the right directions in order to turn on the heating blanket. In this code, the blanket is being turned on and off and you also get the choices of different heat settings on the blanket. You can have a light heat, a medium, heat, a medium hot heat, and then finally a really hot heat based on what you would like to have on your blanket.

This code is pretty simple for what all you will be able to do with it all. You are able to turn on and off the blanket whenever you would like and you have the ability to change the heat setting up and down based on how cold you feel or who is using the blanket. It takes a bit of code writing to get this all to happen, but once the IDE is able to send this code over to the Arduino board, your blanket is ready to work.

And that is all there is to it. Make sure that everything is sewn up properly and then use the blanket whenever you are cold and want to warm up. You may want to be careful with using the really hot setting or it could wear out the board more quickly or can cause too high of heat on your body, but otherwise it will work really great. So snuggle up and enjoy being warm and toasty on those cold and dreary days.

Chapter 9: An Advanced Example of Using the Arduino Board

We have spent some time in this guidebook talking about the benefits of using the Arduino system and some of the projects that you are able to do with it. There is so much that you will be able to create with these boards and if you are looking to create an electronic or robotic project, this is one of the best platforms to use. Here we are going to work on a more advanced project with the LED lights that we are working on before. But instead of just having the lights turn on and off, we are going to use the UNO board in order to use the RGB of the LEDs in order to create a variety of shades of color using just one LED inside.

First, you need to have a few supplies to help you to get started with this project. Some of the supplies that will make things easier include:

A computer that is able to download or install the Arduino IDE.
An Arduino board. We will be using the Arduino UNO board for this example.
A USB cable that will hook into the board and into your computer.
A 4 leg common cathode RGB LED
A basic breadboard
3 22 ohm resistors

Some wires. It is preferable that you get a black, a green, a blue and a red so that you have an easier time getting them to stay in the right places.

For this particular example, we are going to be using the 4-leg RGB LED. The RGB is going to stand for Red, Green, and Blue. With just these three colors, you will be able to generate many other colors for your board. Since this one has four legs, the first one is going to be called the common cathode and then the other three legs will be the ones associated with the three colors on the RGB. The common cathode is the one that is connected to the ground, also known as the GND on the board, while the other three legs will be in need of a 220-ohm resister and they are also going to be tied to the PWM pins.

The colors are going to be varied when you send through different PWM signals to the blue, green, and read leads that are on your LED. So let's get this all set up the right way. Take your black wires and hook them from the first let over to the GND. Notice that this GND will be on the same side of the board as your PWM pins. The RGB LED will have four pins and one of these is going to be a lot longer than all the others; this is the one that will be considered the cathode pin and it is the one that you should connect to your ground.

Next you will take the red wire and place it on the pin 6. We know that this is one of the PWM pins because it as the (~) right beside the number. Then you can take the green wire and place it with the pin 5 and finally the blue wire is going to go with pin 3. The wire colors are going to correspond with the color that the lead goes to.

Now we can move on to the development process. The overall goal is to use this type of LED in order to create some different colors. The input for this project is not going to be required but the output will be the PWM signals that are used to vary the colors that go through with the RGB LED. In addition, the processing will be the type of signal, which will need to be varied by the board in order to produce the different colors that you want.

Next is the design. There are a few things that you should have in place for the design to make sure that it works properly including:
Equipment: you will need the common cathode for the RGB LED as well as 3 of the 220-ohm resistors.
Voltage source: to make this work, you will need a voltage source, which in this case is going to be the PWM pins.
Ground: this is going to be the GND pin that is found on the Arduino board. You will be able to find it on the digital side of our board.
Once you have everything done up to this point, it is time to work on building your prototype on the breadboard.

Now it is time to work with the algorithm. You will first need to work with the initialization which is going to set the constants in order to represent which of your pins is red, which one is green, and which one you set as blue. You can then set it up so that the green, blue, and red pins are ready for the PWM output. Finally, you need to set up the loop so that it will cycle through all of the colors in your sketch while adjusting the output of the PWM using repetition cycles.

This is a lot of information to take in all at once so let's take a look at how all of it will come together in your sketch. If you have already gone through and hooked up the wires in the correct manner that we discussed above, and you make sure that your board is hooked up to the computer, you will be able to type in this sketch in order to get the program to work:

```
int redPin = 6;
int bluePin = 3;
int greenPin = 5;
const int maxVal = 255;
const int minVal = 0;

void setup(){
        pinMode(redPin, OUTPUT);
        pinMode(bluePin, OUTPUT);
        pinMode(greenPin, OUTPUT);
}

void loop() {
        for (int i = 255; i>0; i=i-5){
        for (int j = 255; j>0; j=j-5){
        for (int k = 255; k>0; k=k-5){
        analogWrite(redPin, i);
```

```
        analogWrite(bluePin, j);
        analogWrite(greenPin, k);
        delay(100);
}
}
}
}
```

So at this point, take some time to write this code into your compiler and then let it upload. Make sure that the Tools...Port is set up in the correct way so that the right message is able to be sent through to the board without issues. At this point, the RGB LED should be working in the proper manner, but you should go through and test and debug it to make sure that your circuit is working the way that you expect.

Understanding the Code

We had a lot of information that went through the code that we wrote above and you may be uncertain what it all means or how it is going to work. Let's take some time to look through the code to understand what happened and why all of the parts are so important:

```
int redPin = 6;
int bluePin = 3;
int greenPin = 5;
const int maxVal = 255;
const int minVal = 0;
```

With this first part, we are declaring and initializing some constants and variables. The word "const" means that the variable that is going to follow is not allowed to change values while your program is running. The maxVal is then set to 255 because this is the maximum amount of signal strength that we are able to send to the PWM analog on these pins. For example, if you set the redPin to be 255, you are going to get red and if you set the bluePin to 255, it will be blue. You can't really go stronger than the full on color so that is the highest amount that you will allow on this project.

```
void setup(){
        pinMode(redPin, OUTPUT);
        pinMode(bluePin, OUTPUT);
        pinMode(greenPin, OUTPUT);
```

With this second part of the code, you are working on the setup section of the code. This is the one that is going to run each time that you turn on the board. It is responsible for assigning the digital pins that are connected to the green, blue, and red RGB LED pins that are going to be set for the output. You need to put this part of the code in to ensure that the pins are all set up to take on the job that they should.

```
void loop() {
        for (int i = 255; i>0; i=i-5){
        for (int j = 255; j>0; j=j-5){
```

```
        for (int k = 255; k>0; k=k-5){
        analogWrite(redPin, i);
        analogWrite(bluePin, j);
        analogWrite(greenPin, k);
        delay(100);
}
}
}
}
```

And finally, we will talk about the last part of the code. This is the section that is going to cycle through all the different colors that are in the board. It is going to use three of the repetition structures that we talked about before, the for loops, in order to cycle through a variety of combinations that include green, blue, and red. The delay command that we added into this will keep the color there for 100 ms so that you are able to see them.

Once you have set up this code and are able to see what all it can do, make sure to experiment with it a bit. See if you are able to change some of the values around and see if it will change the number of colors that you are getting. Keep ahold of the original copy in some place safe in case you would like to start over without having to rewrite the whole thing.

At this point, you have finished this more advanced code and gotten the board to show up a wide variety of colors. This one is similar to the LED light that we discussed in an earlier chapter, but now you get to bring in a few more parts and see a variety of colors show up on the board with the help of just three main ones and the right LED board!

Chapter 10: Making a Laser Game with the Arduino UNO

In this chapter, we are going to look at making another project with the help of our arduino UNO board. We are going to work on making our very own laser game which is going to work with the lights and the LEDs that we have worked on in other projects in this book, but it is going to make it into more of a game so it is more fun!

There are a few supplies that we will need in order to get started with our own laser game. Some of the supplies that you will need include:

Lots of wires
Rotry potentiometer
Piezo busser
A resistor
Light dependent resistor
1 blue LED
4 orange LEDs
4 red LEDs
3 green LEDs
The arduino UNO board

Once you have all of the parts, it is time to put it all together. For the lED, you are going to place it with the ports 2, 3, 4, and the ground.

The red is going to go into the ports 8, 9, 10, 11, and ground and the blue is gong to go into port 12 and the ground.

For the others, you will take the resistor that is light depending and place it into the port 3..3V and A3. The resistors don't need to worry about going into the ground. Then the rotry potentiometer will need to go into the port A4 and the ground while the buzzer will need to go into the port 6, make sure that it goes in between the buzzer and the input, and then into the ground.

Now that you have placed all of these in the right locations, let's take a look at what you are doing. The green lights are going to be considered your 3 hearts. You are going to lose a life when you aren't fast enough while trying to hit the target in this game.

With the orange and red lights, you will be able to figure out if the target is hittable. They are going to turn on at times that are random and you will be able to work on hitting the target until your lights all go out.

Then with the blue LED, yu will see that it turns on as soon as you are able to hit one of the targets. Your buzzer is important as well because it is going to make a sad kind of sound when you loose one of your lives, but it will also create a nice happy sound if you are succesful in hitting our target. And then with the potentiometer, you will be able to change how sensitive the target is.

Now you are ready to write out the code and get it to all work for your needs. The code that you will need to use in order to set up your new laser game includes:

```
//set up all the variables:
int readytarget = 300;
int timing = 2000;
int recharge = 2000;
int sensorPin = A0;
int sensorValue = 0;
int led = 8;
int led2 = 9;
int led3 = 10;
int led4 = 11;
int hitLed0 = 12;
int hitLed = 2;
int hitLed2 = 3;
int hitLed3 = 4;
int health = 0;
bool hit = false;
const int buzzer = 6;
```

```
// the setup routine runs once when you press reset or turn on the LEDs:
void setup() {
```

```
pinMode(buzzer, OUTPUT);

// initialize the digital pin as an output:
Serial.begin(9600);
pinMode(led, OUTPUT);
pinMode(led2, OUTPUT);
pinMode(led3, OUTPUT);
pinMode(led4, OUTPUT);
pinMode(hitLed0, OUTPUT);
pinMode(hitLed, OUTPUT);
pinMode(hitLed2, OUTPUT);
pinMode(hitLed3, OUTPUT);
digitalWrite(hitLed, HIGH);
digitalWrite(hitLed2, HIGH);
digitalWrite(hitLed3, HIGH);
}


void sensor(){ //this is the part of the program that senses the light
sensorValue = analogRead(sensorPin);
if(sensorValue > 400){ //change the number to increase/decrease
sensitivity
digitalWrite(hitLed0, HIGH);
tone(buzzer,1500);
delay(200);
tone(buzzer,1000);
delay(200);
tone(buzzer,1500);
```

```
delay(200);
noTone(buzzer);
//blink LEDs in response to high light level
digitalWrite(led, LOW);
digitalWrite(led2, LOW);
digitalWrite(led3, LOW);
digitalWrite(led4, LOW);
delay(recharge);
digitalWrite(hitLed0, LOW);
hit = true;
}
else{
digitalWrite(led, LOW);
}

if (health == 1) {
digitalWrite(hitLed, LOW);
digitalWrite(hitLed2, HIGH);
digitalWrite(hitLed3, HIGH);
}

if (health == 2) {
digitalWrite(hitLed, LOW);
digitalWrite(hitLed2, LOW);
digitalWrite(hitLed3, HIGH);
}
if (health == 3 ) {
```

```
digitalWrite(hitLed, LOW);
digitalWrite(hitLed2, LOW);
digitalWrite(hitLed3, LOW);
 }
}


// the loop routine runs over and over again forever
void loop() {

if (health > 0 and health < 2) {
tone(buzzer,700);
delay(200);
tone(buzzer,500);
delay(200);
tone(buzzer,250);
delay(300);
noTone(buzzer);
 }

if (health > 2 and health < 4) {
tone(buzzer,700);
delay(200);
tone(buzzer,500);
delay(200);
tone(buzzer,250);
delay(300);
noTone(buzzer);
```

```
}

 if (health > 4 and health < 6) {
tone(buzzer,500);
delay(200);
tone(buzzer,250);
delay(200);
tone(buzzer,100);
delay(400);
noTone(buzzer);
}

if( hit == true){
  hit = false;
}
delay(random(1000,10000));

digitalWrite(led, HIGH);
digitalWrite(led2, LOW);
digitalWrite(led3, LOW);
digitalWrite(led4, LOW);
delay(readytarget);
sensor();
 if( hit == true){
  return;
}
 digitalWrite(led, HIGH);
```

```
digitalWrite(led2, HIGH);
digitalWrite(led3, LOW);
digitalWrite(led4, LOW);
delay(readytarget);
sensor();
 if( hit == true){
  return;
}
digitalWrite(led, HIGH);
digitalWrite(led2, HIGH);
digitalWrite(led3, HIGH);
digitalWrite(led4, LOW);
delay(readytarget);
sensor();
 if( hit == true){
  return;
}
digitalWrite(led, HIGH);
digitalWrite(led2, HIGH);
digitalWrite(led3, HIGH);
digitalWrite(led4, HIGH);
delay(timing);
sensor();
 if( hit == true){
  return;
}
digitalWrite(led, LOW);
```

```
digitalWrite(led2, LOW);
digitalWrite(led3, LOW);
digitalWrite(led4, LOW);
(health = health + 1);
delay(readytarget);
sensor();


}
```

Now this code is a bit longer so take your time to get it written out and make sure that all the parts are in the right place. As you start to play the game there are parts that you may want to change, such as working with getting the target a bit easier or harder to catch, but as a beginner, using this code will make it easier to work on the game and to get to playing before long!

Chapter 11: Tips and Tricks When Using Arduino

For those who are not used to working with any coding or programming languages, it may seem like a big undertaking to get started with the Arduino platform. There are some people who are really good at programming, but those are the people who have been working in coding for a long time and probably wouldn't need to use this book. On the other hand, for those who have never used these kinds of codes before, you may be a bit confused about how you get started and worried that you won't be able to figure all of this out.

As a beginner, you will find that Arduino is one of the easier programming languages for you to learn how to use, and if you have worked with the C++ language at all in the past, you will find that this is even easier to accomplish. Even without experience in another programming language, this is a simple coding language that you will be able to learn and it will work well on many different electrical projects so it is really a great one to get into if this is the stuff you want to work on.

Both beginners and experts enjoy using the Arduino platform because it has all the simplicity that a beginner is looking for while also coming with a lot of power that many of your projects are going to need. You will need to make sure that the right IDE is set up inside of your computer and that you are picking out the right boards for each project (there are some options available to make sure that you are picking out the one that you need for your project.

As mentioned, many beginners are worried that learning how to use this language is going to be too difficult, especially if they have never worked with coding in the past. We are going to look at some of the most common complaints that come from beginners who are starting this platform and some tips and tricks to make it a big easier.

First, you should take some precautions when you are picking out the board that you want to use with this program. There are many boards that you will be able to find when you go to purchase them, but each of them are a bit different and will work on different projects depending on what you would like to do. For example, some are going to be embedded and won't have the programming interface that you are looking for, meaning that you will have to purchase this interface separately if you would like to do the programming; in most cases the programming interface will be there, but do take some time to look in case it isn't there. Some boards will need to work with the 5V while others will be fine with a 3.8V battery and there are many other changes that you could find with the Arduino board you are working with.

The board that you will need to pick is going to be based on the project that you are working on. You should take a look at the project that you want to work on and determine which board is going to make it easier to get the project done. For some beginner projects, the type of board will be listed, which can make it easier to create your project while learning about the different options. Later on, you will find that it is easier to determine the boards on your own.

When you first get started with the Arduino platform, you need to take some time to set up your IDE. This is an open sourced language, so you will be able to download the Arduino IDE for free. You will also get the benefit of using the library that comes with the IDE for free, while also making any changes that you need to make your project work the right way.

If you don't take the time to get the IDE set up properly, you are going to have some trouble writing out the code. Your board is not going to respond unless the IDE is up and running for you. It only takes a few minutes to get this to run the right way for you so take that time and get it all set up, and also look through the library so that you can familiarize yourself with how this is going to work.

If you find that you are getting stuck on one of your projects along the way, a good thing to do is go online and find one of the communities or forums that work with the Arduino platform. Here you will be able to ask questions about your projects, look up different information that could help you, or watch some tutorials. There are so many ways that you can get your questions answered if you just go and look around for some advice.

For this guidebook, we started out with some of the basics and showed you a few of the projects that you are able to work with inside of the Arduino system. As you progress through with some more complex programs, you may find that you will need t o use the Logic and Processing parts that come with your system.

When you are working with the Logic part, you need to remember that your module will be able to pick up on two different types of signals; the digital signal and the analog signal. The digital signal is the one that you can make by using a button or a trigger. With the Arduino coding language, the ON button is basically going to be registered as high and the off is the one that is read as low.

In addition, you can also work with the analog signal and you will notice that these are going to work similar to what you find in a dimmer knob. This is when the signals will no longer be simply on or off. You can also separate these out numerically using the numbers 0 to 1023 and this will also vary based on what you need to have done on your project.

Now we can take a look at the Processing part and this is where things sometimes get a bit more complicated. When you are working your way through the Arduino system, you need to keep in mind a few different kinds of specs. For example, you will need to watch out for the components and make sure that their rates match. It is also important that you take the readings from the right port. These will make it easier to send out many different types of sensor values and it is really worth your time to learn how to read these ports and learn how many bytes that you can send out since it will make the process of parsing out data later a bit easier.

When you are looking for a simple way to bring the worlds of electronics and programming together, you are going to find that no other product is going to work like Arduino is. This platform is really easy to learn, whether you have experience with this kind of thing or not, and you will enjoy all the power that comes with it to create some of your own projects. Use the examples of projects in this guidebook and look at the tips in this chapter to learn how to work on Arduino and create some amazing projects of your own.

Conclusion

Thank for making it through to the end of *Arduino: The Essential Step by Step Guide to Begin Your Own Projects*, let's hope it was informative and able to provide you with all of the tools you need to achieve your goals whatever it may be.

The next step is to pick out which project you would like to get started on. The Arduino platform is easy to work with and once you pick out the board that you would like to use as well as get the free IDE set up on your computer, you will be able to get started with your first project.

This guidebook has listed out some of the steps that you need to take in order to get started with some of your first projects. We spent some time talking about the basics of this system and then moved on to how to hook this up to your computer, how to try a few basic projects to get the hang of how this will work for you, and then moved on to writing a few of your own projects that can make working with the Arduino board so much more fun than before.

When you are ready to start learning a new coding language or you want to make sure that you are able to work with your own robotics or electronic projects, make sure to read through this guidebook and learn how you can work with the Arduino platform.

Finally, if you found this book useful in anyway, a review on Amazon is always appreciated!

www.ingramcontent.com/pod-product-compliance
Lightning Source LLC
Chambersburg PA
CBHW071303050326
40690CB00011B/2512